I0007921

EXPLORING

PALWORLD

A Comprehensive Guide to the Ultimate Adventure

MATTHEW H. LARSEN

Copyright

All rights reserved. No part of this publication may be reproduced, distributed, or transmitted in any form or any means, including photocopying, recording or other electronic or mechanical methods, without the prior written permission of the publisher, except in the case of brief quotations embodied in critical reviews and certain other non-commercial uses permitted by copyright law.

Copyright © (Matthew H. Larsen), (2024).

About the Author

There is a famous author named Matthew H. Larsen who writes about video games. He brings a special mix of knowledge and love to the pages of "Exploring PALWORLD: A Comprehensive Guide to the Ultimate Adventure." Matthew has always been interested in video games and virtual worlds. He was born and raised in San Francisco, a city that is very tech-savvy. His early experiences with classic RPGs and adventure games gave him a deep knowledge of how games work and how to tell a story.

Matthew has both academic knowledge and real-world experience in the game business. He has a degree in Game Design from the University of California, Los Angeles. He has helped make both small, independent games and big, popular games while working for some of the best game companies. His writing style, which is both useful and interesting, shows that he knows a lot about how to make games, keep players interested, and use interactive storytelling.

Matthew is very involved in the game community in ways that go beyond his job. He regularly posts on a number of gaming sites and blogs, where he talks about and analyses the newest gaming trends and releases. His ability to connect with other gamers on these sites has made him a recognised voice among gamers.

"Exploring PALWORLD" is more than just a guide; it shows how much Matthew wants to improve players' game experiences. His comprehensive understanding of PALWORLD's mechanics, combined with his ability to convey complex ideas in an accessible way, makes this guide an invaluable resource for both new and seasoned players.

In addition to his gaming interests, Matthew is an advocate for using games in educational settings. He regularly talks at conferences and workshops about the potential of video games as learning tools, stressing how they can develop problem-solving skills and creativity.

When he's not exploring virtual worlds or writing about them, Matthew likes hiking, photography, and playing the piano. His diverse hobbies and continuous pursuit of knowledge are what make him not just a remarkable author, but also an inspiring figure in the gaming community.

Table of Content

Introduction to PALWORLD

What is PALWORLD?

PALWORLD is a captivating and innovative game that has caught the imagination of players worldwide. It is a unique blend of adventure, survival, and creature collection, set in a vast, open-world setting. In PALWORLD, players start on an extraordinary journey where they can capture, train, and care for a wide array of creatures known as "Pals". These Pals are not just companions; they play an important part in various aspects of the game, including combat, crafting, building, and exploration.

The game stands out for its dynamic ecosystem, where players deal with diverse biomes and weather systems. The day and night cycle in PALWORLD adds a realistic touch, affecting the gameplay and behavior of creatures. Players can participate in a range of activities, from battling and taming wild Pals to constructing their own bases and crafting items for life. The multiplayer part of PALWORLD allows for cooperative and competitive play, creating a rich social experience.

The Vision and Inspiration Behind PALWORLD

The idea behind PALWORLD was to create an immersive world that blends the thrill of exploration and discovery with the joy of nurturing and growing with your Pals. The game draws inspiration from various genres and themes, combining aspects of classic creature-collecting games, survival adventures, and open-world exploration.

At its core, PALWORLD is motivated by the human connection with nature and the animal kingdom. The game's creators sought to build a universe where players could not only start on adventures and face challenges but also form meaningful bonds with their Pals. This idea is central to the gameplay, as the relationship between a player and their Pals is crucial for success in the game.

Moreover, PALWORLD's development was driven by a desire to push the boundaries of traditional game genres. The integration of survival features, such as crafting and resource management, into a creature-collecting framework, offers a fresh and engaging experience. This fusion of genres supports strategic thinking and creativity, making each player's journey through PALWORLD unique.

The game's vivid and diverse world, filled with mysterious lands and hidden secrets, aims to evoke a feeling of wonder and adventure. The creators of PALWORLD were motivated by various cultural myths, legends, and natural landscapes, creating a rich tapestry of environments for players to explore.

In essence, PALWORLD is more than just a game; it's a world teeming with possibilities and adventures, intended to capture the hearts of players who love exploration, creatures, and the thrill of discovery.

Getting Started in PALWORLD System

Requirements and Installation Guide
System Requirements:

Before diving into the world of PALWORLD, it's important to ensure your system meets the necessary requirements for a smooth gaming experience. Here are the suggested and minimum system specifications:

Minimum Requirements:

- Operating System: Windows 10 64-bit
- Processor: Intel Core i5 or similar
- Memory: 8 GB RAM
- Graphics: NVIDIA GeForce GTX 660 or similar

- DirectX: Version 11
- Storage: 20 GB unused space
- Internet: Broadband internet service

Recommended Requirements:

- Operating System: Windows 10/11 64-bit
- Processor: Intel Core i7 or similar
- Memory: 16 GB RAM
- Graphics: NVIDIA GeForce GTX 1060 or similar
- DirectX: Version 12
- Storage: 20 GB available space (SSD recommended)
- Internet: High-speed broadband internet link

Installation Guide:

Purchase and Download:

PALWORLD can be purchased and downloaded from major digital distribution platforms such as Steam or the Epic Games Store.

Install the Game:

- Once purchased, add PALWORLD to your library and start the download.
- Follow the on-screen directions for installation. The installer will guide you through the process, including picking an installation directory.

Update Drivers:

Ensure that your graphics card and sound drivers are up to date for best performance.

Launch the Game:

- After installation, open PALWORLD from your gaming library.
- The first launch may include extra setup steps, such as configuring settings and accepting terms and conditions.

Creating Your First Character

Choose Your Appearance:

- The character creation screen in PALWORLD offers a variety of customization choices. You can pick your character's gender, skin tone, facial features, hairstyle, and hair color.

Select Starting Apparel:

- Choose your initial clothes and accessories. While these do not impact gameplay greatly, they add to your character's personality.

Assign Basic Attributes:

- Depending on the game's version, you might have the option to give basic attributes or skills. These could influence your original gameplay experience.

Name Your Character:

- Choose a name for your character. This name will be how other players identify you in the game world.

Introductory Tutorial:

- Most players will gain from going through the introductory tutorial. It offers a quick overview of the basic controls, game mechanics, and beginning steps in PALWORLD.

First Steps in PALWORLD:

- Once your character is made, you'll start in a beginner-friendly area. This zone is meant to ease new players into the game's world, with initial quests and a safe environment to explore the basic mechanics of PALWORLD.

Remember, the trip in PALWORLD is as unique as your character. Feel free to play with different looks and attributes to create an avatar that truly represents your adventure style!

Basic Controls and Interface Overview

Basic Controls in PALWORLD:

Movement:

- WASD: Standard moving keys.
- Spacebar: Jump.
- Shift: Sprint.

Interaction:

- E: Interact with items or characters.
- Right Click: Aim or secondary move.

- Left Click: Primary move or attack.

Inventory and Management:

- I: Open inventory.
- Tab: Access character menu or crafting choices.
- Esc: Open the main menu for settings and game choices.

Communication:

- Enter: Open chat window.
- F1-F4: Quick access to emotes or predefined texts.

Interface Overview:

1 Health and Stamina Bars: Located usually at the bottom or top of the screen, showing your character's current health and stamina.

2 Mini-Map: A small map that gives a quick overview of your immediate surroundings. It often shows icons for key places and characters.

3 Inventory Screen: Accessed by pressing "I", this screen shows all the items you have gathered, your equipment, and crafting materials.

4 **Pal List:** A special interface element that shows your collected Pals, their health, and state.

6 **Quest Log**: This section shows your ongoing quests, objectives, and progress.

7 **Communication Panel:** For multiplayer interactions, including chat and team details.

Understanding these controls and interface elements will greatly improve your initial experience in PALWORLD, allowing you to explore the game world and interact with its elements effectively.

Understanding the PALWORLD Environment

The Diverse Biomes of PALWORLD

PALWORLD offers an incredibly rich and varied environment, characterized by its diverse biomes. Each biome offers unique challenges, landscapes, and opportunities for adventure. Understanding these biomes is crucial for players to effectively explore the world and interact with the different creatures and resources found within them.

Forests and Woodlands:
- Dense with trees and rich in wildlife.
- Home to a variety of Pals, especially those that thrive in wooded areas.

- Resources include wood, herbs, and certain minerals.

Grasslands and Plains:

- Vast open areas with tall plants and scattered trees.
- Ideal for meeting roaming Pals and large herbivores.
- Rich in materials like fibers and certain types of food.

Deserts and Arid Regions:

- Hot, dry places with sparse vegetation.
- Inhabited by Pals adapted to high heat and scarce water.

- Key resources include unique minerals and specific flora.

Mountains and Highlands:

- Rugged land with steep slopes and rocky outcrops.
- Home to tough, mountain-dwelling Pals.
- Sources of rare minerals and materials for crafts.

Tropical Rainforests:

- Lush, thick, and full of life.
- Abundant in exotic Pals and rich plants.
- Plentiful tools, but often challenging to navigate.

Frozen Tundras and Polar Regions:

- Extreme cold regions with snow and ice.
- Inhabited by Pals adapted to cold settings.
- Resources are scarce but can include rare things.

Aquatic Environments (Lakes, Rivers, Oceans):

- Diverse range of aquatic biomes, each with its unique environment.
- Home to a wide range of aquatic and amphibious Pals.
- Resources include fish, watery plants, and special minerals.

Mystical and Unique Biomes:

- Special areas with unique, sometimes magical traits.
- Home to rare and often strong Pals.
- Sources of unique tools and materials not found elsewhere.

Each of these biomes not only offers different Pals and supplies but also presents unique environmental challenges, such as extreme weather conditions, difficult terrains, and unique puzzles or obstacles. Players need to adapt their strategies, equipment, and Pals based on the unique characteristics of each biome to thrive and explore successfully.

Weather Patterns and Environmental Effects

PALWORLD's dynamic weather system adds a layer of realism and difficulty to the gameplay. The weather patterns not only change the visual landscape but also have real effects on the game mechanics.

Rain:

- Can be a light shower or a heavy rain.
- Affects visibility and the actions of certain Pals.
- Can benefit farming tasks but may hinder exploration and combat.

Sunshine and Clear Skies:

- Ideal for exploring and engaging in outdoor sports.
- Boosts the morale of Pals and can enhance certain skills.

Fog:

- Reduces vision significantly.
- Makes stealth easier but navigation more difficult.

Storms and Lightning:

- Can be dangerous, with possible lightning strikes.
- Affects Pals' behavior, with some getting anxious or scared.

Snow and Cold Weather:

- Slows down moving and can affect health if unprepared.
- Certain Pals grow in these conditions, while others may need protection.

Wind:

- Impacts ranged fighting and flying Pals.
- Can also affect the spread of fire in the environment.

Each weather condition requires players to adapt their strategies, from changing travel plans to using different Pals for various jobs. Weather also works with the game world, changing the growth of plants, the availability of certain resources, and the emergence of specific Pals.

Day and Night Cycle: What You Need to Know

The day and night cycle in PALWORLD is not just a cosmetic feature; it greatly influences gameplay.

Daytime:

- Better visibility for exploration and fighting.
- Certain Pals are more active and easy to find.
- Ideal for gathering supplies and engaging in social interactions.

Nighttime:

- Reduced vision, necessitating the use of torches or other light sources.
- Some Pals only appear at night or display unique behaviors.
- Greater chance of encountering hostile creatures.

Impact on Pals and Activities:

- Some Pals may have enhanced skills at night, while others may need to rest.
- Certain quests and missions might only be available or easier to finish during specific times of the day.

Strategic Planning:

- Players need to plan their activities according to the time of day, taking into account the strengths and flaws of their Pals.

Aesthetic and Immersive Experience:

- The changing light and surroundings create an immersive and dynamic world, enhancing the overall gaming experience.

In PALWORLD, the interplay between different weather patterns and the day-night cycle creates a live, breathing world that pushes players to be adaptable and strategic in their approach to exploration, combat, and creature interaction.

The Inhabitants of
PALWORLD

A Guide to PAL Creatures: Types, Habitats, and Behaviors

PALWORLD is home to an interesting array of creatures known as PALs. Each type of PAL has its own unique traits, habitats, and behaviors, making the world of PALWORLD incredibly diverse and engaging. Understanding these creatures is important for players to thrive in the game.

Types of PAL Creatures:

1   **Elemental PALs:** These PALs are associated with specific elements like fire, water, earth, or air. They hold abilities

related to their elements and are often found in environments that match their nature.

2 **Mystical PALs:** Rare and often powerful, these PALs possess powers that seem magical or otherworldly. They are usually found in hidden or hard-to-reach areas.

3 **Combat PALs:** Specially adapted for battles, these PALs have strong offensive and defence powers. They are ideal for players focused on combat.

4 **Resource PALs:** Useful for gathering and crafting, these PALs can help collect materials or assist in building and farming jobs.

5 **Utility PALs:** These PALs have special abilities like healing, transportation, or giving light, making them indispensable for various tasks and exploration.

Habitats of PAL Creatures:

- Each type of PAL is usually found in an environment that fits its characteristics. For example, aquatic PALs are found in water bodies, while desert PALs are located in arid areas.

- Some PALs are migratory and can be found in different habitats based on the season or weather conditions.

Behaviors of PAL Creatures:

1 Social Behavior: Some PALs are social and prefer to be in groups, while others are private.

2 Diurnal and Nocturnal: Like the real world, some PALs are active during the day (diurnal), and others are active at night (nocturnal).

3 Aggressive vs. Passive: Players will meet both aggressive and passive PALs. Understanding their nature is important for successful interaction, whether it's for taming or combat.

4 Special Abilities and Traits: Each PAL has special abilities and traits that can be harnessed by the player. For instance, some may have special skills for fighting, while others can aid in resource collection or exploration.

Interacting with PAL Creatures:

- Players can tame, train, and care for their PALs, forming a bond that improves the PALs' abilities and loyalty.

- Proper care, including feeding and attending to the needs of PALs, is important for maintaining their health and effectiveness.

Adaptation and Evolution:

- Some PALs can adapt or evolve based on their environment, the way they are cared for, or the jobs they frequently perform.

By understanding the various types of PAL creatures, their habitats, and behaviors, players can carefully approach how they interact with, capture, and utilize these creatures in their PALWORLD adventures.

Interacting with Pals: Taming, Training, and Caring

In PALWORLD, interacting with Pals is a core part of the gameplay. Taming, training, and caring for these creatures are important to your success and enjoyment in the game.

Taming Pals:

- **Approach**: Each Pal has a unique character. Some may require a gentle approach, while others might need to be subdued or inspired.

- **Feeding**: Offering special foods can help in taming certain Pals. Knowing their chosen diet is key.

- **Special things:** Some Pals may require specific things or conditions to be tamed, like special baits or environmental factors.

Training Pals:

- **Skill Development**: Training your Pals enhances their abilities, whether it's for combat, resource gathering, or other jobs.

- **Bonding**: Spending time with your Pals and participating in activities together strengthens your bond, unlocking new skills and abilities.

- **Customized Training:** Tailor your training strategies to the unique traits and potential of each Pal.

Caring for Pals:

- **Health and Well-being**: Regularly feed and care for your Pals to keep them healthy. Neglect can lead to lower effectiveness or even illness.

- **Habitat Maintenance**: Creating a suitable living situation for your Pals is important, especially for those with specific habitat needs.

- **Emotional Care:** Pay attention to the emotional state of your Pals. Happy and happy Pals perform better and are more loyal.

The Role of NPCs: Allies, Enemies, and Quest Givers

Non-Playable Characters (NPCs) in PALWORLD play various roles, greatly enhancing the game's depth and storyline.

Allies:

- Allies are friendly NPCs who can help you in your journey. They might give support in battles, provide valuable information, or trade resources.

- Building relationships with allies can lead to collaborative ventures and open special quests or items.

Enemies:

- Enemy NPCs offer challenges and obstacles. They can range from rival adventurers to members of opposing groups.

- Engaging with enemies often leads to combat situations and takes strategic planning to overcome.

Quest Givers:

- Quest Givers are NPCs who give tasks or missions. These quests can range from simple collection jobs to complex adventures involving exploration and combat.

- Completing quests given by these NPCs can yield rewards such as resources, equipment, or new Pals.

- Quests also drive the storyline, showing more about the world of PALWORLD and its mysteries.

Interacting with both Pals and NPCs in PALWORLD provides a dynamic and immersive experience. Understanding and successfully managing these interactions is key to exploring the full depth of the game.

Gameplay Mechanics and Strategies

Exploration and Adventure: Tips for Surviving the Wilderness

Exploring the vast wilderness of PALWORLD is a core part of the game experience. The wilderness can be both wondrous and dangerous, so here are some important tips to help you live and thrive during your adventures.

Prepare Adequately:

- Gather Supplies: Before heading out, stock up on necessary supplies like food, water, healing items, and tools.

- Equip Proper Gear: Wear suitable clothing and armor based on the biome you're exploring. Different environments may require unique gear.

Understand the Biome:

- Each biome in PALWORLD has unique traits and challenges. Familiarize yourself with the terrain, weather patterns, and types of Pals and supplies available.

Stay Alert:

- Keep an eye on your surroundings for possible dangers, such as aggressive Pals or environmental hazards.

- Listen to audio cues; sometimes, you can hear danger before you see them.

Travel with Pals:

- Pals can be invaluable companions in the wilderness, giving aid in combat, navigation, and resource gathering.

- Choose Pals that complement your exploration style and the unique challenges of the biome.

Use the Day/Night Cycle to Your Advantage:

- Plan tasks like travel and resource gathering during the day for better visibility.

- Nighttime can be used for stealthier activities or to meet nocturnal Pals.

Conserve Resources and Energy:

- Manage your supplies wisely. Overloading yourself can slow you down and drain your energy faster.
- Use materials sparingly and try to replenish them from the environment whenever possible.

Learn Basic Survival Skills:

- Skills like building a shelter, starting a fire, and finding food and water are important for extended exploration trips.

Map Your Journey:

- Keep track of your travel route. Marking important places and resources on your map can be incredibly helpful.

Adapt to Weather and Environmental Changes:

- Be prepared to change your plans or take shelter during harsh weather conditions.

Stay Healthy:

- Monitor your health and energy. Rest and recuperate when necessary to keep peak condition.

Engage with the Environment:

- Interact with different factors in the environment, such as flora and fauna. These interactions can yield valuable resources or knowledge.

Learn from Experience:

- Each exploration venture is a chance to learn. Pay attention to what works and what doesn't, and adjust your tactics accordingly.

Crafting and Building: A Step-by-Step Guide

Crafting and building in PALWORLD are important skills that allow players to create tools, structures, and items necessary for survival and progress. Here's a step-by-step guide to get you started:

Gather Resources:

- Collect basic materials like wood, stone, fibers, and metals from your surroundings.

- Different biomes offer unique resources, so explore different areas.

Learn Recipes and Blueprints:
- Unlock or find recipes for crafting items and building structures.

- Recipes can be learned from finishing quests, exploring, or interacting with NPCs.

Use the Crafting Menu:
- Access the crafting menu to see what items you can make with your present resources.

- This menu will also show you what extra materials you need for items you can't yet craft.

Start with Basic Tools:

- Create basic tools like axes, pickaxes, and hammers which will allow you to gather more varied and advanced materials.

Build a Shelter:

- Your first big crafting project should be building a shelter. This will provide safety and a place to store things.

- Start with a simple structure and expand it as you gather more materials.

Crafting for Survival:

- Make important survival items like clothes, weapons, and cooking tools.

- Don't forget to make storage units to keep your inventory organized.

Experiment and Customize:

- As you progress, experiment with different crafting combinations to make unique items.

- Personalize your buildings to fit your needs and aesthetic preferences.

Combat and Defense: Mastering Skills and Tactics

Combat in PALWORLD is a thrilling and challenging element of the game. Mastering fighting skills and methods is crucial for defending against hostile creatures and enemies.

Understand Your Weapons:

- Familiarize yourself with the various weapons available and understand their strengths and flaws.

- Different weapons are designed for different combat styles and situations.

Utilize Pals in Combat:

- Some Pals are skilled at combat and can be crucial allies in battle.

- Understand your Pals' skills and how they can complement your fighting style.

Learn Enemy Patterns:

- Observe and learn the attack patterns of foes and hostile Pals.

- Anticipating attacks can help you dodge and counter successfully.

Use the Environment:

- Use environmental elements for cover, ambushes, or to escape.

- Environmental hazards can sometimes be used to your advantage in battle.

Develop Your Skills:

- Improve your character's fighting skills through training and practice.

- Skill points can often be allocated to improve combat effectiveness.

Balance Offense and Defense:

- Mastering the timing between hitting and defending is key.

- Know when to press the attack and when to fall back and protect.

Keep Health and Resources in Check:

- Ensure you have enough health potions and recovery items during battle.

- Manage your stamina so you don't run out of energy at a key moment.

Adapt Tactics to Different Opponents:

Different enemies may require different tactics. Adapt your methods based on who or what you are facing.

By honing your crafting and building skills and mastering battle and defense tactics, you will be well-prepared to face the challenges and adventures that await in the world of PALWORLD.

Quests and Missions

Understanding Quest Types: Story, Side, and Hidden Quests

In PALWORLD, quests and missions are integral to the gameplay, giving players a structured way to experience the game's narrative, explore its world, and gain rewards. There are several types of quests, each with its unique traits and rewards.

Story Quests:
- Purpose: Story quests are the backbone of PALWORLD's story. They progress the main storyline and often feature important characters and events.

- Features: These quests generally have a set sequence and are designed to gradually increase in difficulty, guiding players through the game.

- Rewards: Completing story quests often unlocks new areas, features, or powers, and gives substantial rewards.

Side Quests:

- Purpose: Side quests are optional tasks that delve into side stories or additional challenges. They offer a better understanding of the game's world and characters.

- Variety: These quests can range from simple chores like gathering resources to complex adventures involving puzzles or combat.

- Flexibility: Players can usually finish side quests at their own pace and in any order, providing a break from the main storyline.

Hidden Quests:

- Discoverability: Hidden quests are not clearly marked on the map or quest log. They require exploration or interaction with specific objects or NPCs to be found.

- Challenge: These quests often involve unique challenges or puzzles and may take more effort to complete.

- Rewards: Hidden quests can offer unique and valuable rewards not found in other quest types, making them useful for those who seek them out.

Tips for Managing Quests:

1 Track Your Progress: Keep an eye on your quest log to track current quests and their objectives.

2 Prioritize: Depending on your playstyle, you may choose to focus on story quests to advance the plot or take on side quests for additional exploration and rewards.

3 Explore Thoroughly: Take the time to explore the environment thoroughly, as this can lead to finding hidden quests.

4 Balance Quest Types: Balancing your focus between story, side, and hidden tasks can provide a well-rounded experience and prevent the gameplay from becoming monotonous.

Engaging with the different types of quests in PALWORLD enriches the gameplay experience, offering a blend of narrative development, exploration, challenge, and reward.

Strategies for Completing Missions Successfully

Successfully completing missions in PALWORLD takes strategy, preparation, and sometimes a bit of creativity. Here are some useful strategies:

Understand the Mission Objectives: Before starting, fully understand what is needed to complete the mission. This includes the major objectives, any secondary goals, and the conditions for success.

Plan Your Approach: Depending on the mission type, plan your method. Whether it involves combat, exploration, or puzzle-solving, having a plan in place can make a big difference.

Equip Appropriately: Tailor your equipment and inventory to the task. This might mean bringing specific weapons, tools, or things that will be useful.

Use Pals Effectively: Choose Pals that complement the mission's needs. Their abilities can be important in certain situations.

Manage Resources Wisely: Keep an eye on your supplies, including health, stamina, and materials. Running out of necessary tools mid-mission can lead to failure.

Learn from Failed Attempts: If you fail a mission, analyze what went wrong and adjust your strategy properly.

Stay Alert and Adaptable: Be prepared to adapt your strategy on the fly, as unexpected challenges can appear during a mission.

Rewards and Achievements: Maximizing Your Gains

Completing tasks in PALWORLD not only progresses your journey but also brings various rewards and achievements. Here's how to maximize these gains:

Complete Bonus Objectives: Many missions have secondary goals that, when achieved, offer extra rewards.

Aim for Efficiency: Completing tasks efficiently, such as within a time limit or with minimal resource usage, can sometimes yield better rewards.

Explore Thoroughly: Often, missions will have hidden areas or secret items that can be found through careful exploration.

Collect Everything: Don't leave resources or things behind. Even if they don't seem useful instantly, they could be valuable later.

Track Achievements: Keep an eye on the game's award system. Completing certain goals or challenges often rewards players with unique items or bonuses.

Replay Missions: Some missions can be replayed for extra rewards or to earn a higher ranking.

Multiplayer and Social Aspects

Engaging with the PALWORLD Community: Social Features Explained

PALWORLD offers a rich multiplayer experience with various social features that allow players to connect with the community, cooperate, and compete with others. Understanding and utilizing these tools can greatly improve your gaming experience.

Cooperative Gameplay:

- Team Up: Join forces with friends or other players to explore, finish missions, and battle together.
- Shared Goals: Work towards common objectives, such as building big structures or taking down powerful enemies.

Competitive Play:

- PvP (Player vs. Player): Engage in battles against other players to test your skills and tactics.
- Leaderboards: Compete for top spots in different challenges and missions.

Trading and Economy:

- Trade with Players: Exchange resources, Pals, and things with other players.

- Participate in the Economy: The in-game economy allows players to buy, sell, and trade goods, adding to a dynamic marketplace.

Communication Tools:

- Chat Systems: Use in-game chat for real-time contact with other players.

- Voice Chat: Some platforms may offer integrated voice chat for more immersive cooperation.

Guilds and Communities:

- Join or Create a Guild: Being part of a guild offers a sense of community and opens up opportunities for guild-specific tasks and activities.
- Community Events: Participate in events organized by the game or player groups for unique experiences and rewards.

Social Spaces:

- Hub Areas: Specific areas in the game are built as social hubs where players can meet, interact, and plan activities.
- Show Off Achievements: Use these spaces to showcase your achievements, Pals, or creations.

Friend Systems:

- Add Friends: Build a friends list for easy grouping and conversation.
- Visit Friends' Worlds: Some versions of PALWORLD may allow you to visit your friends' bases or regions.

Collaborative Building and Crafting:

- Work Together: Engage in large-scale building or crafting projects that require teamwork and resource pooling.

Community Feedback and Involvement:

- Participate in Forums and Discussions: Share your experiences, provide comments, and stay informed about game updates and community news.

Engaging with the PALWORLD community through these social features not only improves the fun but also opens up new dimensions of gameplay, from collaborative projects to competitive challenges.

Cooperative (co-op) gameplay in PALWORLD offers an enriching experience where players can team up with friends to explore, finish missions, and engage in various activities together.

Forming a Team:

- Invite friends or other players to start a group.

- Teams can consist of people with different skills and Pal types, allowing for a balanced and strategic approach to challenges.

Shared Missions and Objectives:

- Undertake missions that are especially designed for co-op play, with objectives that require teamwork.

- Share the rewards and progress achieved through these tasks.

Exploring Together:

- Navigate through the diverse biomes of PALWORLD with your team, sharing findings and tackling obstacles together.

- Coordinate with your team to utilize different Pals and abilities successfully.

Building and Crafting:

- Engage in building projects where each team member provides resources and skills.

- Collaborate on crafting items that help the whole team.

Strategy and Communication:

- Effective communication is key in co-op play, whether it's through in-game chat or external voice conversation tools.

- Plan and execute strategies together, combining your skills and Pals for the best outcomes.

Competitive Play: Tournaments and Player vs Player (PvP) Challenges

Competitive play in PALWORLD adds an exciting edge to the game, allowing players to test their skills against others in different formats.

PvP Battles:

- Engage in player vs player action, either in one-on-one duels or team-based battles.

- Test your combat plans and skills against other players in real-time.

Tournaments:

- Participate in organized tournaments, which can range from small-scale local competitions to big, server-wide events.

- Tournaments often have unique rules and objectives, offering a different challenge from regular gameplay.

Leaderboards and Rankings:

- Compete for top spots in various categories, such as fastest task completion, highest combat scores, or most Pals captured.

- Leaderboards support a competitive spirit and provide recognition for outstanding performances.

Seasonal and Special Events:

- Special events or seasonal competitions offer unique challenges and rewards, often with a limited time to join.

Fair Play and Balance:

- The game's competitive system is meant to match players of similar skill levels, ensuring fair and enjoyable matches.

Whether teaming up with friends for cooperative adventures or diving into the thrill of competitive play, PALWORLD offers a diverse and engaging multiplayer experience that caters to different playstyles and tastes.

Customization and Personalization

Character Customization: Appearance, Skills, and Gear

In PALWORLD, character customization allows players to create and change their avatar to reflect their personal style and gameplay preferences.

Appearance:

- Customize physical traits such as face shape, skin tone, hair style, and color.

- Select from a variety of clothing choices to create a unique look.

Skills:

- Choose and develop skills that match your chosen playstyle, whether it's combat, crafting, or exploration.

- Skill choices can change how you interact with the environment and Pals.

Gear:

- Equip gear like weapons, armor, and tools, which not only change your look but also provide specific gameplay benefits.

- Gear can often be upgraded or modified to increase its attributes.

Pal Customization: Unique Traits and Abilities

Customizing your Pals in PALWORLD is important for maximizing their potential and making them truly yours.

Unique Traits:

- Each Pal can have unique traits that can be improved or modified through training and care.

- Some traits are innate, while others can be formed over time.

Abilities:

- Train your Pals to develop special abilities that aid in combat, exploration, or resource gathering.

- The abilities of your Pals can complement your character's skills, making a more effective team.

Aesthetic Customization:

- Customize the appearance of your Pals with different accessories or color changes, adding a personal touch.

Building Your Home Base: Personalization Tips and Tricks

Creating and personalizing your home base in PALWORLD is not only a fun feature of the game but also an important strategic element.

Location Selection:

Choose a location for your base considering things like resource availability, proximity to key areas, and environmental conditions.

Layout and Design:

Plan the layout of your base for speed and aesthetics. Consider having separate areas for crafting, storage, Pal habitats, and personal space.

Resource Management:

Gather and manage resources efficiently to build and grow your base.
Use local materials to give your base a unique style that fits with the biome.

Defense and Security:

Incorporate defensive elements like walls, traps, and lookout places to protect your base from hostile creatures and people (in PvP areas).

Personal Touches:

Add personal touches with decorative items, furniture, and unique building features.
Create themed areas or rooms that show your interests or achievements in the game.

Expand and Upgrade:
Continuously grow and upgrade your base as you progress in the game. Newer and better materials and technologies can be added as you discover them

Advanced Gameplay and Endgame Content

Challenges and Boss Fights: Preparing for the Ultimate Tests

As players progress in PALWORLD, they face more challenging aspects of the game, including tough challenges and boss fights. Here's how to prepare for these ultimate tests:

Upgrade Gear and Skills:

- Ensure your gear is top-notch and your skills are honed to their best potential.
- Consider gear and skills that are especially effective against the bosses you'll face.

Understand Boss Mechanics:

- Study the bosses' attack routines and weaknesses.

- Each boss usually has a unique set of moves and weaknesses.

Gather Intelligence:

- Use community tools, such as forums or guides, to gather tips and strategies on defeating tough bosses.

Stock Up on Resources:

- Have a sufficient supply of healing items, buffs, and other required consumables.

Team Up Strategically:

- For multiplayer boss fights, team up with other players whose skills and Pals match yours.

Endgame Content: Exploring High-Level Areas and Activities

Endgame content in PALWORLD offers experienced players difficult and rewarding activities:

High-Level Areas:

- Explore areas that are meant for high-level players, with tougher enemies and more complex puzzles.

- These areas often hold rare resources and unique Pals.

Special Quests and Missions:
- Undertake challenging quests and missions that are only open at higher levels.
- These often involve intricate storylines and high-reward situations.

Elite Crafting and Building Projects:
- Engage in crafting and building projects that take rare materials and advanced skills.

Participate in High-Level Tournaments and Events:

- Compete in events and tournaments that are especially designed for top-tier players.

Continuous Development: Updates and Future Expansions

PALWORLD is a game that grows over time, with developers continuously working on updates and expansions:

Regular Updates:

- Stay updated with regular patches and updates that may bring new features, improvements, and bug fixes.

Future Expansions:

- Look forward to expansions that add new places, Pals, quests, and features to the game.

Community Feedback:

- The development of PALWORLD often considers community feedback, so staying involved in the community can give you a voice in future content.

Stay Informed:

- Keep an eye on official announcements, developer diaries, and community channels for news on future material.

Troubleshooting and Community Resources

Common Issues and How to Resolve Them
Playing PALWORLD, like any complicated game, can sometimes lead to encountering issues. Here are some common problems and their possible solutions:

Game Crashes or Freezes:

- Check if your system meets the minimum needs.

- Update your graphics drivers and ensure your running system is up to date.

- EVerify the game files through the platform you got it from (e.g., Steam).

Connection Problems:

- Ensure your internet link is stable.

- Restart your router/modem.

- Check for any server-related issues mentioned by the game developers.

Performance Issues (Lag, Low FPS):

- Lower the game's graphics settings.

- Close unnecessary background apps.

- Check for overheating problems with your hardware.

In-Game Bugs or Glitches:

- Report the bug to the developers through official methods.

- Check online forums to see if others have encountered the same problem and if there are any known workarounds.

Getting Help: Community Forums and Support Channels

If you need assistance or want to learn more about PALWORLD, different resources are available:

Official Forums:

A place to discuss the game, share experiences, and seek help from other players.

Social Media and Online Communities:

Platforms like Reddit, Discord, and Twitter often have busy PALWORLD communities.

Support Channels:

For technical help, use the official support channels provided by the game's developers.

Game Guides and Wikis:

Utilize internet guides and wikis for detailed information about the game's mechanics, items, Pals, and strategies.

Contributing to the PALWORLD Community

Being an active member of the PALWORLD community can improve your gaming experience and that of others:

Participate in Discussions:

Share your experiences, tips, and tactics in forums and social media groups.

Create Content:

If you're into content creation, try making guides, videos, or streams to help and entertain other players.

Provide Feedback:

Constructive comments to the developers can help improve the game. Participate in surveys or feedback threads if applicable.

Help Others:

Assist new players with tips or help them in-game, fostering a welcoming and supportive community.

Stay Informed and Involved:

Keeping up with updates and news helps you to stay informed and contribute relevant and current information to discussions.

By troubleshooting effectively, utilizing community resources, and actively adding to the PALWORLD community, players can enjoy a more enriching and connected gaming experience.

Conclusion

Final Thoughts and Tips for Ongoing Adventures

As you delve into the captivating world of PALWORLD, here are some final thoughts and tips to improve your ongoing adventures:

Explore and Experiment:

- Be curious and discover every corner of PALWORLD. The game is rich in secrets and surprises waiting to be found.

- Experiment with different methods, Pals, and playstyles to find what works best for you.

Stay Engaged with the Community:

- The PALWORLD community is a useful resource. Engage with fellow players for tips, friendship, and shared experiences.

Balance Your Play:

- While it's easy to get absorbed, remember to balance your gameplay with real-life tasks. Healthy gaming habits ensure long-term pleasure.

Embrace Challenges:

- Challenges are chances for growth in PALWORLD. Don't be discouraged by setbacks; use them as learning lessons.

Keep Updated:

Stay updated about game updates, expansions, and events to make the most out of your PALWORLD experience.

The Future of PALWORLD: What's Next?

The trip in PALWORLD doesn't end. Here's what to look forward to:

Continuous Updates:

Regular updates will bring new features, improvements, and bug fixes, keeping the game fresh and interesting.

Upcoming Expansions:

Anticipate expansions that bring new biomes, Pals, quests, and storylines.

Evolving Gameplay:

As the game matures, expect to see evolving gameplay mechanics and richer material.

Community-Centric Developments:

The developers of PALWORLD have shown a commitment to listening to the community, so player comments will likely shape future developments.

Emerging Technologies:

Keep an eye out for the integration of new technologies and trends in gaming that could improve the PALWORLD experience.

PALWORLD is a dynamic, ever-evolving world filled with endless potential. Whether you're exploring uncharted areas, taming and training Pals, or engaging in epic battles, each day brings a new adventure. So gear up, gather your Pals, and start on your journey in the mesmerizing world of PALWORLD!

www.ingramcontent.com/pod-product-compliance
Lightning Source LLC
LaVergne TN
LVHW051710050326
832903LV00032B/4121